The Bread

From Genesis to Revelation

Osvaldo Feliciano

The Bread

From Genesis to Revelation

Osvaldo Feliciano

"I am the bread of life: he that cometh to me shall never hunger;

and he that believeth on me shall never thirst."

—John 6:35

Legacy Publishing House

Copyright Page

The Bread: From Genesis to Revelation

* * *

Scripture quotations, unless otherwise indicated, are taken from the King James Version (KJV).

Published by Legacy Publishing House

Email: infopublishinghouse@gmail.com

First Edition — 2026

Cover Design: Legacy Publishing House

Interior Design and Formatting: Legacy Publishing House

Editorial Development: Legacy Publishing House

Printed in the United States of America.

* * *

Publisher's Note

This book is intended for spiritual growth, biblical study, and inspirational reading. The views expressed are rooted in the authors' biblical convictions and pastoral reflections.

ISBN: 979-8-9958054-3-4

Dedication

This work is dedicated first to the glory of God,

to Jesus Christ, the Bread of Life,

and to every believer hungry for deeper revelation through His Word.

> *"Man shall not live by bread alone, but by every word that proceedeth out of the mouth of God."*
>
> *—Matthew 4:4*

Acknowledgments

First and foremost, all glory and honor belong to God. It was He who placed this desire within my heart — the passion to compose this work in the way that it has been composed. I am grateful for His patience with me throughout this process, and for the divine enlightenment He provided each time I encountered a moment of confusion or uncertainty. Every time I reached a crossroads, He was faithful to inspire me forward, and for that I am eternally thankful.

I also want to give special recognition to my dear friend, Nelson Alonso. Around the year 2016, he spoke a prophetic word over my life — that I would one day write books. Although writing had always been a desire of mine, I could never see myself physically carrying it out; it was one of the most difficult things for me to imagine doing. I am grateful for his obedience to God in delivering that word, because on that day a seed was planted deep in my heart. Today, those seeds have produced fruit, and this book stands as a testimony to what God does when we simply believe.

To my beloved wife, Narcheline Feliciano — you have been an extraordinary help throughout this journey. There were many moments where, without hesitation, you would sit beside me, take the keyboard, and type because I was struggling to get things right on my own. Your consistency, your patience, and the love you have shown toward my dreams and desires have meant more to me than words can express. This book carries your fingerprints, and I thank God for you.

I want to also acknowledge my family — my mother, my father, and my brothers — each of whom has shaped the person I am today. My father, in particular, holds a place of deep honor in my heart. From the time I was a young boy, he instilled the Word of God in me. I can still remember sitting and listening to him teach, using his own children as an audience to rehearse what he had just been reading and studying. He may not have known it at the time, but in doing so, he planted within me an unquenchable love for the Scriptures and a desire to learn and teach the Word of God. For that, I am profoundly and deeply grateful. This book is specifically dedicated to him. I love him with all my heart.

I want to extend my sincere gratitude to my pastors, Pastor Osvaldo Rivera and Pastor María Isabel Rodríguez, for pushing me forward and for the vital role they played in helping me complete and finalize this work. Your encouragement, your spiritual covering, and your investment in my life have been a tremendous blessing.

To my children — thank you for your patience and for allowing me the space and quiet to write this book. You are one of the greatest reasons I press forward.

Finally, to everyone who has touched my life at one point or another — whether through a word of encouragement, an act of service, a season of friendship, or a moment of prayer — your contribution has not gone unnoticed. This book exists, in part, because of each of you. I love you all.

Sincerely and with love,

Amen.

Prologue

The Bread That Tells the Story of Redemption

Bread is one of the simplest elements of human life. It is common, familiar, and found at nearly every table in every culture. Yet in Scripture, bread is never just bread.

From the first pages of Genesis to the final invitation in Revelation, bread carries a divine message. It tells the story of humanity's fall, our daily dependence, our spiritual hunger, and God's relentless plan to redeem us.

Bread first appears in the shadow of the curse. After Adam's disobedience, God declared that man would eat bread by the sweat of his brow. What once was effortless provision in Eden became labor, struggle, and the reminder that sin had altered everything.

But even in the curse, God planted a promise.

Throughout Scripture, bread begins to transform:

- In the wilderness, it falls from heaven as manna.
- In Abraham's tent, it becomes hospitality and covenant.
- At David's table, it becomes grace that covers brokenness.
- In Joseph's story, it becomes provision in famine.
- In Bethlehem, the House of Bread, it becomes flesh.

Jesus did not simply give bread—He became bread.

He became the Bread of Life for a hungry world:

- Bread for the weary
- Bread for the sinner
- Bread for the broken
- Bread for the searching soul

This book is an invitation to trace the golden thread of redemption through one of the Bible's most powerful symbols. It is a journey from labor to rest, from curse to blessing, from temporary provision to eternal satisfaction.

May every chapter draw you deeper into the heart of the One who said:

> *"I am the bread of life: he that cometh to me shall never hunger."*
>
> ***—John 6:35***

Introduction

The Bread: From Genesis to Revelation

Bread is perhaps the most universal food known to humanity—simple, sustaining, and present at tables across generations and nations. Yet in Scripture, bread is never merely food. It carries profound theological significance, appearing as a sacred symbol woven through the entire redemptive story of God.

From the opening chapters of Genesis to the closing vision in Revelation, bread emerges as more than sustenance; it becomes a language through which God reveals divine truths. It speaks of provision in seasons of need, covenant in moments of communion, dependence in times of wilderness, and redemption in the fullness of Christ.

When God declared to Adam, *"In the sweat of thy face shalt thou eat bread"* (Genesis 3:19), bread became tied to the human condition—labor, dependence, and the consequences of the Fall. Yet what first appeared under the shadow of the curse would, through God's unfolding plan, become a symbol of grace.

Throughout Scripture, bread appears repeatedly as part of God's revelation:

manna in the wilderness,

showbread in the Tabernacle,

bread at Abraham's table,

bread in Joseph's storehouses,

bread broken at the Last Supper,

and ultimately Christ Himself declaring:

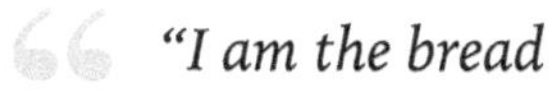

> *"I am the bread of life." (John 6:35)*

In Jesus, bread reaches its fullest meaning. What once symbolized toil becomes rest. What once represented human need becomes divine fulfillment. What once sustained the body becomes, in Christ, nourishment for the soul.

This book traces that sacred thread—from Genesis to Revelation—revealing how God uses something as ordinary as bread to unveil extraordinary truths about covenant, mercy, obedience, communion, sacrifice, and eternal hope.

For the story of bread is ultimately the story of redemption itself.

May these pages invite you to see Scripture with fresh wonder, to recognize the richness hidden in what often seems ordinary, and above all, to encounter Jesus Christ—the true Bread of Life—who alone satisfies the deepest hunger of the human soul.

> *"Blessed are they which are called unto the marriage supper of the Lamb."*
>
> *—Revelation 19:9*

1
By the Sweat of Your Brow
Genesis 3:19 - The Foundation of Human Labor and Sustenance

The Divine Declaration

> *"In the sweat of thy face shalt thou eat bread, till thou return unto the ground; for out of it wast thou taken: for dust thou art, and unto dust shalt thou return."* - *Genesis 3:19 (KJV)*

These words, spoken by the Almighty God to Adam after the Fall, mark one of the most significant moments in human history. Here, in the shadow of humanity's first disobedience, bread is introduced not merely as food, but as the product of toil, the fruit of labor, and the daily reminder of our fallen state.

Before the Curse: Eden's Abundance

To understand the weight of Genesis 3:19, we must first consider what came before. In the Garden of Eden, provision was effortless and abundant. Genesis 1:29 records God's original design: "And God said, Behold, I have given you every herb bearing seed, which is upon the face of all the earth, and every tree, in the which is the fruit of a tree yielding seed; to you it shall be for meat."

Notice what is absent from this original provision: there is no mention of bread, no reference to cultivation, no indication of labor required for sustenance. The earth yielded its fruit freely, and humanity partook of God's provision without sweat, without struggle, without the grinding of grain or the kneading of dough.

The Fall: From Gift to Labor

When sin entered the world through Adam and Eve's disobedience, everything changed. The curse that followed their rebellion fundamentally altered humanity's relationship with both God and creation. The ground that once yielded freely would now resist man's efforts. The food that once grew without labor would now require toil, sweat, and perseverance.

It is significant that God specifically mentions bread in this curse: not fruit, not herbs, not the varied provisions of Eden—but bread. Why bread? It is because bread represents transformed sustenance. Unlike fruit that grows naturally on trees, bread must be made. Grain must be planted, tended, harvested, ground, mixed, kneaded, and baked. Bread is the product of human labor working in partnership with God's provision of seed, soil, sun, and rain.

The Prophetic Nature of Bread

From this first mention in Genesis, bread becomes prophetic. It speaks of humanity's condition: we are dependent beings who must work for our sustenance, yet we cannot create life from nothing. We can plant and tend, but only God can make the seed grow. We can grind and bake, but only God can transform grain into nourishment for the body.

This dependence is not merely physical but spiritual. Just as man cannot live without bread for the body, he cannot live without spiritual sustenance from God. The physical hunger that drives us to labor for bread mirrors the spiritual hunger that should drive us to seek God.

Bread as Daily Reminder

The daily nature of bread consumption makes it a constant reminder of our dependence. Unlike other foods that might be consumed occasionally, bread was (and remains) a staple food consumed daily. Each time the Israelites ate bread, they were reminded of their fallen state and their need for God's provision.

This daily reminder served multiple purposes:

1. **Humility:** Remembering that sustenance comes through labor, not by right
2. **Dependence:** Acknowledging that even with labor, success depends on God's blessing
3. **Mortality:** Recognizing that physical sustenance is temporary—we labor for bread until we "return unto the ground"
4. **Hope:** Pointing forward to a greater provision that would come through God's redemption

The Sweat of the Brow

The phrase "sweat of thy face" (or "sweat of your brow") has become synonymous with hard work and honest labor. But in its original context, it represents something far more profound than mere physical exertion. It represents the cosmic shift that occurred when sin entered the world.

The Hebrew word for "sweat" here is זֵעָה (ze'ah), which can mean perspiration but also carries connotations of anxiety and trouble. This suggests that humanity's labor for bread would be marked not only by physical effort but by mental and emotional strain. The simple act of obtaining daily bread would become fraught with uncertainty, difficulty, and concern.

Foreshadowing the Greater Provision

Even in this curse, we can see the seeds of redemption. The very fact that God provides a way for humanity to obtain sustenance—even if through labor—demonstrates His mercy. He could have decreed that no food would satisfy human hunger, but instead, He established a system where human effort, combined with His provision, would meet physical needs.

More importantly, this verse foreshadows the coming of One who would reverse the curse. Jesus Christ, the second Adam, would not only provide spiritual bread but would also bear the curse of labor and death on behalf of humanity. When Christ declared Himself to be "the bread of life" (John 6:35), He was offering what Adam's labor could never truly provide: bread that satisfies eternally and requires no sweat of the brow to obtain.

The Universal Human Condition

Genesis 3:19 describes not just Adam's fate, but the universal human condition. Every person born into this world inherits the necessity to labor for bread. Rich or poor, educated or simple, every human being must work in some form to sustain life. Even those who do not physically bake bread must labor to obtain the means to purchase it.

This universal condition serves God's purposes in several ways:

1. **It levels humanity:** All people, regardless of status, share the common need for daily bread.
2. **It creates community:** The complexity of bread-making often requires cooperation and division of labor.

3. **It teaches dependence:** No individual is completely self-sufficient; we depend on farmers, millers, bakers, and ultimately, God.
4. **It builds character:** Honest labor for daily bread develops qualities like perseverance, responsibility, and appreciation.

Theological Implications

The theological implications of Genesis 3:19 extend far beyond the simple need for food. This verse establishes several crucial doctrines:

The Doctrine of Work: Labor is not a result of industrialization or capitalism—it is part of

God's design for humanity after the Fall. Work has dignity because it is ordained by God as the means by which humanity obtains sustenance.

The Doctrine of Providence: While humans must labor, the success of that labor depends entirely on God's provision. He provides the rain, the sunshine, the fertile soil, and the strength to work.

The Doctrine of Mortality: The phrase "till thou return unto the ground" reminds us that physical life, sustained by physical bread, is temporary. This creates a natural longing for something more permanent, more satisfying.

The Doctrine of Redemption: The very difficulty of obtaining bread points to humanity's need for a better provision, a bread that satisfies eternally.

The Hebrew Understanding

For the Hebrew people, bread held special significance that went beyond mere nutrition. The Hebrew word for bread, לֶחֶם (lechem), comes from a root meaning "to fight" or "to wage war," suggesting the struggle involved in obtaining sustenance. This struggle was not seen as merely physical but as spiritual—a daily battle against the forces that would prevent God's people from receiving His provision.

In Hebrew culture, bread was so central to life that the word lechem was often used to refer to food in general. When the Psalms speak of God providing food (lechem) for the hungry, they are speaking of bread as the representative of all sustenance.

Looking Forward

As we begin this journey through Scripture's teachings on bread, Genesis 3:19 provides our foundation. Here we learn that bread is not merely food—it is a daily reminder of our fallen state, our dependence on God, and our need for redemption. Every meal becomes a theological statement, every bite of bread a confession of our creatureliness.

Yet this is only the beginning.

As we trace bread through the Biblical narrative, we will discover how God transforms this symbol of curse into a symbol of blessing, this reminder of our mortality into a promise of eternal life, and this product of human labor into a gift of divine grace.

The story of bread in Scripture is ultimately the story of redemption itself—how God takes the most basic human need and uses it to reveal the deepest spiritual truths. From the sweat-earned bread of Genesis to the freely given Bread of Life in the Gospels, we will see how God's grace transforms curse into blessing, labor into rest, and death into life.

2

MANNA - "WHAT IS IT?"

EXODUS 16 - GOD'S HEAVENLY BREAD AND THE LESSON OF OBEDIENCE

From Curse to Grace: A Divine Reversal

ONE OF THE most fascinating subjects in the entire Bible is the account of manna in the wilderness. It is crucial to keep in mind that bread, as established in Genesis 3:19, was a direct result of the Fall. Before sin entered the world, humanity was free to eat fruit and vegetables without labor. But after the Fall, we were condemned to work and sweat for our daily bread—this too is thoroughly Biblical.

Now we find ourselves in the book of Exodus, where a dramatic reversal of the curse takes place. Israel is wandering in the desert, crying out to God for food, and in His mercy, God provides something unprecedented: bread from heaven that requires no human labor to produce.

The Divine Command and Provision

God gave Moses a remarkable command, promising to provide bread directly from heaven:

> *"Then said the LORD unto Moses, Behold, I will rain bread from heaven for you; and the people shall go out and gather at a certain rate every day, that I may prove them, whether they will walk in my law, or no.*

And it shall come to pass, that on the sixth day they shall prepare that which they bring in; and it shall be twice as much as they gather daily." - Exodus 16:4-5 (KJV)

> *"And when the children of Israel saw it, they said one to another, It is manna: for they wist not what it was. And Moses said unto them, This is the bread which the LORD hath given you to eat." - Exodus 16:15 (KJV)*

"I Know Not What This Is"

The Hebrew word "manna" literally means, "What is it?" When the Israelites first saw this heavenly provision, their immediate response was bewilderment: they could not explain what it was because it came from heaven. This divine mystery is profound —here was bread that no baker could make, no store could sell, and no human effort could produce.

Think about the contrast: when you need regular bread, you must gather ingredients, work the dough, knead it, bake it, and then you have bread. In our modern times, you can go to any store and purchase whatever bread you desire. But manna? Manna could not be found in any marketplace, created in any bakery, or produced by any human baker. Only God was capable of making manna.

Divine Instructions and Perfect Obedience

Unlike regular bread that simply required work to obtain, manna came with precise divine instructions that demanded perfect obedience:

1. **Daily Portion Only:** You could only take

enough for that day, or else it would rot and breed worms (Exodus 16:20).

2. **Double on the Sixth Day**: On the sixth day, they were to gather twice as much because the seventh day was the Sabbath.
3. **No Gathering on Sabbath:** On the seventh day, there would be no manna to gather—it was a day of rest.

This was unique in every way because this bread had a specific function. It wasn't like regular bread where you worked to receive it; instead, this bread required your absolute obedience to follow God's instructions to the letter.

A Prophetic Foreshadowing

This manna system beautifully foreshadows the end times. We are living in the "sixth day" of God's plan, and He is giving out more than normal —extra provision for those who are obedient. Only the obedient ones are receiving this extra measure, because on the "seventh day", there will be no more manna. The seventh day represents the day of rest, the day we all gather together and rejoice in God's amazing work on the cross.

The Mystery of Divine Provision

"I don't know what this is!" This declaration is amazing because it reveals a profound truth: we think we must understand everything God gives us, but we don't. We simply need to be obedient and trust Him. The manna represented something beyond human comprehension—a direct intervention of the divine into the natural order.

Freedom from the Curse

The manna was monumentally important because, for the first time since the Fall, Israel did not have to worry about the curse of working and sweating for their bread. God was providing once again, wanting to re-establish with Israel what He had once established with Adam in Eden—effortless provision from a loving Creator.

Yet despite this incredible grace, Israel grew discontent. They became greedy and wanted to return to Egypt to eat onions, garlic, and meat. God had provided everything they needed, yet they cried out for their past bondage, not understanding the significance of what they possessed.

Understanding Purpose vs. Understanding Provision

Not understanding what manna was is one thing, but not understanding your purpose is quite another. The Israelites failed to grasp that God was teaching them dependence, obedience, and trust. The manna they received daily would keep them alive not just for today, but for tomorrow as well. It was a daily lesson in faith—trusting God for tomorrow's provision while being faithful with today's portion.

The Perpetual Memorial

The significance of manna was so great that God commanded it to be preserved as a memorial:

> *"And Moses said, This is the thing which the LORD commandeth, Fill an omer of it to be kept for your generations; that they may see the bread wherewith I have fed you in the wilderness, when I brought you forth from the land of Egypt." - Exodus 16:32 (KJV)*

This manna was stored in the Tabernacle alongside Aaron's rod and the tablets of the Law—three powerful symbols of God's provision, authority, and covenant.

The Showbread: Consistent Divine Presence

God also commanded that, in the Tabernacle, there should be bread consistently present—not just any bread, but twelve fresh loaves at all times:

> *"And thou shalt set upon the table shewbread before me alway." - Exodus 25:30 (KJV)*

This showbread (literally "bread of the Presence") represented the twelve tribes of Israel constantly before God. It teaches us that it is necessary to have consistent spiritual nourishment in our churches, homes, and personal lives. We cannot survive on sporadic spiritual feeding any more than we could survive on sporadic physical meals.

David's Hunger and Holy Bread

Even King David, when desperately hungry, ate the showbread from the Tabernacle (1 Samuel 21:6). This incident, later referenced by Jesus, shows us that genuine spiritual hunger justifies partaking of holy provision. We must always be ready, constantly prepared to receive what God provides, whether it comes in familiar forms or as mysterious as manna—"What is it?"

The Greater Lesson

The manna teaches us several crucial truths:

1. **God can suspend His own curse**: Even though mankind was condemned to labor for bread, God can provide without human effort.
2. **Obedience is required**: Divine provision comes with divine instructions that must be followed precisely.
3. **Daily dependence:** We cannot stockpile God's grace; we need fresh provision each day.
4. **Mystery is acceptable:** We don't need to understand everything God gives us: we need to trust and obey.
5. **Present provision sustains future hope:** Today's manna gives strength for tomorrow's journey.

From Manna to the Bread of Life

The manna was a temporary provision for a temporary journey, but it pointed to something eternal. When Jesus declared, "I am the bread of life" (John 6:35), He was offering what manna could only symbolize—spiritual sustenance that satisfies eternally, bread from heaven that never spoils, and provision that requires no human labor but demands complete faith and obedience.

Just as the Israelites had to trust God daily for their manna, we must trust Christ daily for our spiritual sustenance. Just as manna came with specific instructions, following Christ requires precise obedience to His word. Also, just as the Israelites often failed to appreciate the miracle of manna, longing instead for the familiar foods of Egypt, we, too, can fail to appreciate the miracle of Christ's provision, longing instead for the familiar but inferior things of this world.

The question "What is it?" should drive us not to skepticism but to worship, recognizing that our God specializes in providing what no human effort can produce, what no earthly source can supply, and what no finite mind can fully comprehend.

3
ABRAHAM'S TABLE - BREAD OF HOSPITALITY AND COVENANT

GENESIS 18 - WHEN HEAVEN COMES TO DINNER

The Transformation of Bread's Purpose

FROM THE SWEAT-EARNED bread of Genesis 3 and the miraculous manna of Exodus, we now encounter bread taking on an entirely new dimension in the life of Abraham. Here, bread becomes more than sustenance or even divine provision—it becomes a sacred medium of hospitality, blessing, and a covenant relationship with God Himself.

This transformation is profound: bread evolves from a reminder of our fallen condition to an instrument of divine fellowship. In Abraham's tent, we witness the beginning of something far more magnificent in the Christian life—bread as a moment of hospitality, blessing, and a covenant communion.

Abraham: The Hospitable Patriarch

Abraham was renowned for his hospitality, and according to Biblical tradition, he positioned himself at the entrance of his tent specifically to welcome travelers and strangers. This wasn't merely cultural courtesy—it was a spiritual discipline, a way of life that reflected his heart toward both God and humanity.

The Bible records that Abraham consistently met people at the door of his tent, ready to offer refreshment, rest, and fellowship. This practice revealed something beautiful about the patriarch's character: he understood that every encounter with another human being was an opportunity to serve God.

The Divine Visitation

The most extraordinary example of Abraham's bread-centered hospitality occurs in Genesis 18, when three mysterious visitors appeared at his tent:

> *"And the LORD appeared unto him in the plains of Mamre: and he sat in the tent door in the heat of the day; And he lift up his eyes and looked, and, lo, three men stood by him: and when he saw them, he ran to meet them from the tent door, and bowed himself toward the ground, And said, My Lord, if now I have found favour in thy sight, pass not away, I pray thee, from thy servant: Let a little water, I pray you, be fetched, and wash your feet, and rest yourselves under the tree: And I will fetch a morsel of bread, and comfort ye your hearts; after that ye shall pass on: for therefore are ye come to your servant. And they said, So do, as thou hast said." -Genesis 18:1-5 (KJV)*

The Sacred Meal Preparation

What follows is one of the most beautiful hospitality scenes in all of Scripture. Abraham doesn't merely offer bread—he orchestrated an elaborate feast:

> *"And Abraham hastened into the tent unto Sarah, and said, Make ready quickly three measures of fine meal, knead it, and make cakes upon the hearth. And Abraham ran unto the herd, and fetcht a calf tender and good, and gave it unto a young man; and he hastened to dress it. And he took butter, and milk, and the calf which he had dressed, and set it before them; and he stood by them under the tree, and they did eat." - Genesis 18:6-8 (KJV)*

Notice the urgency and excellence in Abraham's preparation. He didn't offer ordinary bread but instructed Sarah to use "fine meal"—the best flour available. The bread became cakes "upon the hearth," freshly baked with the finest ingredients. This wasn't survival food or even regular sustenance: this was feast bread, celebration bread, covenant bread.

The Divine Identity Revealed

What made this meal transcendent is the gradual revelation of who these guests truly were. This wasn't just human hospitality: this was communion with the Divine. The three men represented the LORD Himself, and Abraham, unknowingly at first, was hosting heaven at his table.

The breaking of bread with these divine visitors established several revolutionary principles:

1. **Heaven Comes to Earth:** God descends to share a meal with humanity.
2. **Bread as Sacred Medium:** Simple bread becomes the vehicle for a divine encounter.
3. **Hospitality as Worship:** Serving others becomes an act of serving God.
4. **Covenant Fellowship:** Shared meals seal divine relationships.

The Beginning of Something Magnificent

This meal marked the beginning of something far more grandeur in the Biblical narrative and in the Christian life. From this moment forward, shared bread becomes associated with:

- **Divine Encounter:** Just as God met with Abraham over bread, He continued to meet with His people through shared meals. This principle echoes throughout Scripture and finds its ultimate fulfillment in Christ's table fellowship.

- **Covenant Relationship:** The meal with Abraham wasn't casual dining—it was covenant-making. During this visit, God reaffirmed His promises about Isaac's birth and Abraham's descendants. Bread becomes the backdrop for God's most sacred commitments.
- **Hospitality as Ministry:** Abraham's example established that offering bread to strangers was offering bread to God Himself. This principle is later echoed by Jesus: "I was a stranger, and ye took me in… Inasmuch as ye have done it unto one of the least of these my brethren, ye have done it unto me" (Matthew 25:35, 40).

The Prophetic Nature of Abraham's Table

Abraham's sharing of bread with divine visitors prophetically foreshadows several New Testament realities:

The Incarnation: Just as God came to Abraham's tent in human form, He would later come to humanity permanently in the person of Jesus Christ.

The Lord's Supper: The intimate fellowship over bread between Abraham and the Divine prefigures Christ's institution of communion, where bread becomes His body given for us.

The Marriage Supper of the Lamb: Abraham's feast points forward to the ultimate banquet in Revelation, where God will feast with His people for eternity.

Daily Fellowship with God: Abraham's practice of hosting strangers teaches us that every meal can be a sacred encounter, every act of hospitality a form of worship.

The Theology of Sacred Hospitality

Through Abraham's example, bread takes on profound theological significance:

Bread as Bridge: Bread becomes the bridge between the human and divine realms. It's earthy enough to satisfy human hunger yet sacred enough to host divine presence.

Bread as Blessing: The bread Abraham offered wasn't just food—it was a blessing made tangible. Through sharing bread, blessing flows from host to guest and back again.

Bread as Covenant: Shared meals in the ancient world established relationships and sealed agreements. Abraham's meal with God literally sealed the covenant promises.

Bread as Community: The bread brought together Abraham, Sarah, the servants, and the divine visitors in one united fellowship. It created a community where none existed before.

The Excellence of Abraham's Offering

Abraham's choice to use "fine meal" for his divine guests teaches us about the quality of our offering to God. He didn't offer leftover bread or second-rate ingredients. When heaven came to dinner, Abraham gave his best.

This principle applies to our spiritual lives: when we offer ourselves to God, when we serve others in His name, when we participate in communion, we should give our finest, not our leftovers. The bread we share should represent the excellence of our devotion.

Sarah's Partnership in Ministry

Sarah's role in preparing the bread was equally significant. She took the fine meal and quickly kneaded it into cakes. This wasn't a solo ministry for Abraham—it was a partnership. Sarah's skilled hands transformed the meal into bread fit for divine consumption.

This partnership model establishes that the hospitality ministry involves the whole household. The bread that blessed the divine visitors was the product of both Abraham's generous heart and Sarah's skilled preparation.

The Standing Service

Genesis 18:8 notes that Abraham "stood by them under the tree" while they ate. Even after having prepared this magnificent feast, Abraham didn't recline and enjoy the meal with his guests. He served. He stood ready to meet their every need.

This detail reveals the heart of true hospitality: it's not about what we receive but what we give. Abraham found his joy not in eating but in watching his guests enjoy the bread he provided. This servant-heart becomes a model for all who would serve God through serving others.

The Lasting Impact

The bread shared in Abraham's tent didn't just satisfy temporary hunger—it changed the course of history. During this meal, God announced that Sarah would conceive Isaac within a year. The bread that hosted this divine promise became part of salvation history.

This teaches us that our acts of hospitality, our shared meals, our offered bread may seem ordinary to us, but they can become extraordinary in God's hands. We never know when our simple hospitality might become the venue for divine intervention.

From Abraham's Tent to Christ's Table

The progression from Abraham's hospitality to Christ's communion is unmistakable:

- Abraham offered bread to divine visitors; Christ offers Himself as bread to us.
- Abraham's bread hosted God's promises; Christ's bread fulfills God's promises.
- Abraham's meal sealed the old covenant; Christ's meal establishes the new covenant.

- Abraham served while his guests ate; Christ serves us the bread of eternal life.

The Challenge of Abraham's Example

Abraham's example challenges every believer to see their table, their home, their shared meals as potential venues for divine encounter. Every act of hospitality becomes an opportunity to host heaven, every piece of shared bread a possible medium for God's blessing.

The question for us is not whether God might come to our table, but whether we're prepared when He does. Are we positioned like Abraham at the tent door, ready to welcome strangers? Do we offer our finest, or do we give only what's convenient? Are we prepared to serve while heaven dines?

The Beginning of Covenant Fellowship

In Abraham's tent, bread transcended its curse-laden origins in Genesis 3 and its miraculous provision in Exodus 16. Here, bread became the foundation of covenant fellowship, the substance of sacred hospitality, and the medium of divine encounter.

This transformation sets the stage for bread's continuing evolution throughout Scripture. From Abraham's tent, bread will continue to serve as a sacred element in divine-human relationships, ultimately finding its complete fulfillment when the Bread of Life Himself sat at the table with tax collectors and sinners, broke bread with disciples, and offered His own body as the ultimate bread of covenant fellowship.

Abraham's table teaches us that hospitality is not merely a social grace: it is a spiritual discipline. Bread is not merely food: it is a sacramental element. And shared meals are not merely social occasions: they are covenant-making, blessing-conferring, divine-encounter-enabling sacred moments.

David's Table: The Legacy of Abraham's Hospitality

The profound tradition of covenant hospitality that began with Abraham found one of its most beautiful expressions centuries later in the life of King David. After Saul's death, when David had finally ascended to the throne of Israel, he demonstrated the same heart of hospitality that characterized Abraham, but with an even deeper dimension of grace and forgiveness.

The Bible records this remarkable account:

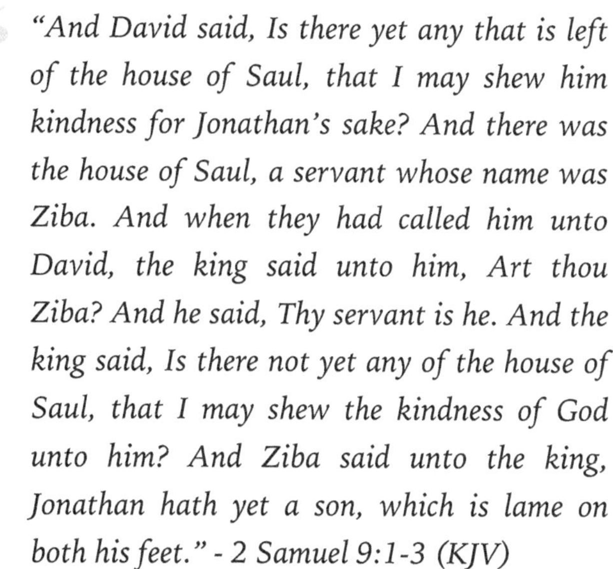

> *"And David said, Is there yet any that is left of the house of Saul, that I may shew him kindness for Jonathan's sake? And there was the house of Saul, a servant whose name was Ziba. And when they had called him unto David, the king said unto him, Art thou Ziba? And he said, Thy servant is he. And the king said, Is there not yet any of the house of Saul, that I may shew the kindness of God unto him? And Ziba said unto the king, Jonathan hath yet a son, which is lame on both his feet." - 2 Samuel 9:1-3 (KJV)*
>
> *"Then king David sent, and fetched him out of the house of Machir, the son of Ammiel, from Lodebar. Now when Mephibosheth, the son of Jonathan, the son of Saul, was come unto David, he fell on his face, and did reverence. And David said, Mephibosheth. And he answered, Behold thy servant. And David said unto him, Fear not: for I will surely shew thee kindness for Jonathan thy father's sake, and will restore thee all the land of Saul thy*

father; and thou shalt eat bread at my table continually." - 2 Samuel 9:5-7 (KJV)

The Irony of Divine Hospitality

This account is profoundly ironic and beautiful. Here was David, the very king whom Saul had relentlessly pursued and tried to kill, now seeking out someone from Saul's house to show kindness to. David practiced the same radical hospitality that Abraham had demonstrated—wanting to show love, compassion, and forgiveness through a meal.

But David's hospitality went even beyond Abraham's. Abraham welcomed divine strangers—David welcomed his former enemy's broken grandson. Abraham hosted the unknown; David invited the unwanted.

Mephibosheth: The Broken Guest

The young man David found was Mephibosheth, Jonathan's son, who had been crippled since childhood.

The Bible explains how this happened:

> *"And Jonathan, Saul's son, had a son that was lame of his feet. He was five years old when the tidings came of Saul and Jonathan out of Jezreel, and his nurse took him up, and fled: and it came to pass, as she made haste to flee, that he fell, and became lame. And his name was Mephibosheth." - 2 Samuel 4:4 (KJV)*

This boy's legs had been broken at a young age when his nurse, fleeing with him after news of Saul and Jonathan's deaths, dropped him in her haste to escape. The physical brokenness of Mephibosheth becomes a powerful symbol of humanity's spiritual condition.

The Table That Covers Our Shame

The most profound aspect of this story was what happened when Mephibosheth sat at David's table.

The Bible records:

> *"So Mephibosheth dwelt in Jerusalem: for he did eat continually at the king's table; and was lame on both his feet." - 2 Samuel 9:13 (KJV)*

When Mephibosheth sat at the king's table, something beautiful happened: the table covered his broken legs. While his disability remained, it was hidden beneath the table. Above the table, he appeared equal to everyone else dining with the king. The table covered the part of him that brought shame, and made him appear whole in the king's presence.

This is a stunning picture of God's grace toward us. We all carry deficiencies, brokenness, and shame. Like Mephibosheth, we have been injured by the Fall: broken by sin, and left unable to walk properly in righteousness. Yet when God invites us to His table, our brokenness is covered. We are made equal with all the other guests at the divine feast.

The Father's Heart for Fellowship

This account reveals something profound about our heavenly Father's heart: God the Father is also looking to eat with us. Just as David sought out someone from his enemy's house to show kindness to, our heavenly Father seeks us out—not because we deserve it, but because of His covenant love.

David's question, "Is there yet any that is left of the house of Saul, that I may show him kindness?" echoes God's heart toward humanity: "Is there yet any among the fallen that I might show grace to?" The answer, thankfully, is always yes.

The Psalm of the Table

This beautiful account brings to mind David's own words in Psalm 23:

> *"Thou preparest a table before me in the presence of mine enemies: thou anointest my head with oil; my cup runneth over." - Psalm 23:5 (KJV)*

David understood what it meant to have a table prepared for him by a gracious host. In showing kindness to Mephibosheth, David was acting out what God had done for him. The table prepared "in the presence of mine enemies" became even more meaningful when we realize that David literally prepared a table for the grandson of his greatest enemy.

From Abraham to David to Christ

The progression of bread's significance continues to unfold:

- **Abraham's table** hosted divine visitors and received covenant promises.
- **David's table** welcomed the broken and extended covenant kindness.
- **Christ's table** will welcome all who come in faith, covering our brokenness with His righteousness.

Each table builds upon the previous one, revealing more of God's character and His redemptive plan. Abraham showed us that God desires fellowship with humanity. David showed us that God extends grace to the undeserving. Christ will show us that God offers eternal communion to all who believe.

The Continuing Legacy

The magnificent thing that began in Abraham's tent, was exemplified in David's palace, continues today whenever believers gather to break bread in Christ's name. Every time we welcome the broken to our tables, every time we show kindness to those who cannot repay us, every time we share our bread with those who have nothing to offer in return, we echo both Abraham's ancient hospitality and David's royal grace.

We participate in the sacred fellowship that began under the oaks of Mamre, was continued in the palace of Jerusalem, and finds its ultimate fulfillment at the table of the Lamb.

4
Joseph, the Bread, and the Wine - A Divine Typology

Genesis 37-41 - From the Pit to the Palace, From Dreams to Reality

The Beloved Son Cast Into the Pit

The story of Joseph began with love and jealousy intertwined. Joseph was the beloved son of Jacob, favored above all his brothers. This favoritism, symbolized by the coat of many colors, stirred such intense envy in his brothers that they plotted against him:

> *"And when they saw him afar off, even before he came near unto them, they conspired against him to slay him. And they said one to another, Behold, this dreamer cometh. Come now therefore, and let us slay him, and cast him into some pit, and we will say, Some evil beast hath devoured him: and we shall see what will become of his dreams." - Genesis 37:18-20 (KJV)*

The brothers threw Joseph into a dry well, then after consideration, decided to sell him instead. They took his precious coat, tore it, put blood on it, and deceived their father Jacob into believing that a wild beast had killed his beloved son. What they intended for evil, God would use for the salvation of nations.

In Potiphar's House: Favor and False Accusation

Joseph was sold to Potiphar, an officer of Pharaoh, and even in slavery, the Lord was with Joseph:

> *"And the LORD was with Joseph, and he was a prosperous man; and he was in the house of his master the Egyptian. And his master saw that the LORD was with him, and that the*

> *LORD made all that he did to prosper in his hand." - Genesis 39:2-3 (KJV)*

Joseph rose to become overseer of Potiphar's entire household. However, his righteousness and integrity led to another trial. Potiphar's wife desired him, and when he refused her advances and fled, leaving his garment in her hands, she falsely accused him of attempting to assault her.

> *"And she caught him by his garment, saying, Lie with me: and he left his garment in her hand, and fled, and got him out. And it came to pass, when she saw that he had left his garment in her hand, and was fled forth, That she called unto the men of her house, and spake unto them, saying, See, he hath brought in an Hebrew unto us to mock us; he came in unto me to lie with me, and I cried with a loud voice." - Genesis 39:12-14 (KJV)*

In Egypt, such an accusation could have easily cost Joseph his life. Yet remarkably, he was not executed but merely imprisoned. This suggests that Potiphar, deep inside, knew Joseph could not have been capable of such an act. Even Potiphar's mercy was orchestrated by God's providence.

The Prison: God's Preparation Ground

In prison, Joseph once again found favor, and God prepared him for his ultimate destiny:

> *"But the LORD was with Joseph, and shewed him mercy, and gave him favour in the sight of the keeper of the prison." - Genesis 39:21 (KJV)*

It was in this prison that one of the most profound typological scenes in all of Scripture unfolds.

The Two Dreams: Bread and Wine

Two of Pharaoh's officers—the chief baker and the chief butler (wine keeper)—were imprisoned and each had a dream:

> *"And the chief butler told his dream to Joseph, and said to him, In my dream, behold, a vine was before me; And in the vine were three branches: and it was as though it budded, and her blossoms shot forth; and the clusters thereof brought forth ripe grapes: And Pharaoh's cup was in my hand: and I took the grapes, and pressed them into Pharaoh's cup,*

and I gave the cup into Pharaoh's hand." - *Genesis 40:9-11 (KJV)*

"When the chief baker saw that the interpretation was good, he said unto Joseph, I also was in my dream, and, behold, I had three white baskets on my head: And in the uppermost basket there were of all manner of bakemeats for Pharaoh; and the birds did eat them out of the basket upon my head." - *Genesis 40:16-17 (KJV)*

The Divine Interpretation

Joseph interpreted both dreams with divine insight:

To the butler: "Yet within three days shall Pharaoh lift up thine head, and restore thee unto thy place: and thou shalt deliver Pharaoh's cup into his hand, after the former manner when thou wast his butler." - Genesis 40:13 (KJV)

To the baker: "Yet within three days shall Pharaoh lift up thy head from off thee, and shall hang thee on a tree; and the birds shall eat thy flesh from off thee." - Genesis 40:19 (KJV)

The contrast is stark and prophetic: the wine

keeper would live, but the bread maker would die in three days.

The Profound Typology

This scene is a divine typology that foreshadows the Last Supper and Calvary. When Jesus instituted the Lord's Supper, He said, "Take, eat: this is my body" (the bread), and "Drink ye all of it; For this is my blood" (the wine) - Matthew 26:26-28.

What was first established in Genesis 3:19—bread as the product of human labor and the reminder of mortality—is now being brought full circle to Jesus' table. The bread maker's death in three days becomes a prophetic shadow of Christ's own death and resurrection.

The typology reveals this truth: bread alone, representing our physical sustenance and human efforts, leads to death. But bread combined with wine—representing both body and blood, both sacrifice and life—leads to eternal life. The spirit is indeed more important than mere physical bread.

Joseph's Request and the Wine Keeper's Forgetfulness

Joseph made a request to the wine keeper:

> *"But think on me when it shall be well with thee, and shew kindness, I pray thee, unto me, and make mention of me unto Pharaoh, and bring me out of this house." - Genesis 40:14 (KJV)*

Yet the Scripture records: "Yet did not the chief butler remember Joseph, but forgot him." - Genesis 40:23 (KJV)

This forgetfulness was part of God's perfect timing. Joseph needed to remain in prison until Pharaoh's own dreams required divine interpretation.

Pharaoh's Dream and Joseph's Elevation

Years later, when Pharaoh had troubling dreams that none of his wise men could interpret, the butler finally remembered Joseph:

> *"Then spake the chief butler unto Pharaoh, saying, I do remember my faults this day:*

> *Pharaoh was wroth with his servants, and put me in ward in the captain of the guard's house, both me and the chief baker: And we dreamed a dream in one night, I and he; we dreamed each man according to the interpretation of his dreams. And there was there with us a young man, a Hebrew, servant to the captain of the guard; and we told him, and he interpreted to us our dreams; to each man according to his dream he did interpret." - Genesis 41:9-12 (KJV)*

When Joseph interpreted Pharaoh's dreams about seven years of plenty followed by seven years of famine, Pharaoh immediately elevated him to second in command over all Egypt.

From the Well to the World's Bread Supply

The divine irony is breathtaking: the brothers who threw Joseph into a well, thinking they were destroying him, had actually pushed him into his purpose. God used their evil intentions to position Joseph exactly where He needed him to be—in charge of all the food in the world.

> *"And Pharaoh said unto Joseph, See, I have set thee over all the land of Egypt... And the famine was over all the face of the earth: And Joseph opened all the storehouses, and sold them unto the Egyptians; and the famine waxed sore in the land of Egypt. And all countries came into Egypt to Joseph to buy corn; because the famine was so sore in all lands." - Genesis 41:41, 56-57 (KJV)*

Every person in the known world had to come to Egypt—to Joseph—just to get grain. The rejected son had become the bread supplier for the world.

The Calvary Connection

The theology here is amazing and powerful. Jesus, like the baker, was falsely accused and had to suffer death. But unlike the baker, Jesus became the Bread of Life. In John's Gospel, Jesus declares: "I am the bread of life: he that cometh to me shall never hunger; and he that believeth on me shall never thirst." - John 6:35 (KJV)

In the Gospel of John, there are seven "I AM" statements of Jesus, and one of the most significant is "I am the bread of life." Jesus died on the cross, but His death was not the end—it was the beginning of His ability to feed the entire world spiritually.

The Threefold Pattern

The pattern of three appears throughout this narrative:

- **In prison:** Joseph, the baker, and the wine keeper (three men)
- **The dreams:** three baskets, three branches, three days
- **At Calvary:** Jesus and two thieves (three crosses)

On the cross, we see the fulfillment of the prison typology:

- **Jesus represents Joseph:** The innocent one who suffers for others' sins.
- **The repentant thief represents the wine keeper:** He asks Jesus to remember him, just as Joseph asked the butler to remember him.
- **The unrepentant thief represents the baker:** He mocks Jesus and faces death without redemption.

When the repentant thief said, "Lord, remember me when thou comest into thy kingdom," Jesus responded just as the wine keeper's dream foretold: "Today shalt thou be with me in paradise" (Luke 23:42-43).

The Resurrection Reality

Once Jesus died and resurrected, He was able to feed the entire world because of His death and resurrection. Just as Joseph became the bread supplier for the physical world during famine, Jesus became the Bread of Life for the spiritual world during humanity's spiritual famine.

The progression is divine:

- Joseph fed the world's bodies with physical bread during physical famine.
- Jesus feeds the world's souls with spiritual bread during spiritual famine.
- Both were rejected by their own people initially.
- Both were elevated to positions where they could save those who had rejected them.
- Both required people to come to them for sustenance.

The Brothers' Return

When Joseph's brothers came to Egypt seeking food during the famine, they unknowingly bowed before the brother they had thrown into the pit. Joseph, now having the power of life and death over them, chose mercy and provision instead of vengeance. This foreshadows how Christ, whom humanity rejected and crucified, now offers salvation to those very people who rejected Him. The Bread of Life welcomes all who come to Him hungry.

The Ultimate Bread Theology

Joseph's story reveals that God's plan for bread extends far beyond physical sustenance:

1. **Bread requires suffering:** Both Joseph and Jesus suffered before becoming bread providers.
2. **Bread comes through death:** The baker died, Joseph "died" to his old life, and Jesus died literally—all leading to bread provision.
3. **Bread brings life:** Joseph's bread saved nations from starvation; Jesus' bread saves souls from spiritual death.

4. **Bread requires elevation:** Joseph had to be elevated to Pharaoh's right hand; Jesus had to be elevated on the cross and then to the Father's right hand.
5. **Bread creates dependence:** All nations depended on Joseph; all humanity must depend on Jesus.

The Completed Circle

From Genesis 3:19's curse of laboring for bread, we now see bread becoming the means of salvation. The very thing that reminded humanity of their fallen state becomes the instrument of their redemption. Joseph's story bridges the gap between cursed bread and blessed bread, between bread earned by sweat and bread given by grace.

The well that was meant to destroy Joseph became the pathway to his purpose. The cross that was meant to destroy Jesus became the pathway to eternal life. Both the pit and the cross were God's methods of positioning His chosen ones to become the bread suppliers for a hungry world.

5
The Last Supper - The Bread of Life Revealed

Matthew 26, Mark 14, Luke 22, John 13-17 - The Ultimate Fulfillment

Born in the House of Bread

THE STORY of Jesus and bread begins even before His birth. Ironically, Jesus was born in Bethlehem, which in Hebrew means "house of bread" (בֵּית לֶחֶם - Beit Lechem). This was no coincidence. When Jesus later declared, "I am the bread of life" (John 6:35), it revealed that His intention had always been to become the very bread mentioned in Genesis 3:19.

When God declared in Genesis that man shall eat bread all the days of his life through the sweat of his brow, His ultimate intention was not to burden humanity permanently, but to create a longing that only He could satisfy. Jesus came to be the bread that humanity was truly in need of.

The Easy Yoke: Reestablishing Eden

Jesus offered a revolutionary alternative to the Genesis curse:

> *"Come unto me, all ye that labour and are heavy laden, and I will give you rest. Take my yoke upon you, and learn of me; for I am meek and lowly in heart: and ye shall find rest unto your souls. For my yoke is easy, and my burden is light." - Matthew 11:28-30 (KJV)*

Instead of working for bread, Jesus says His yoke is easy and His burden is light. He was reestablishing the covenant relationship that God had with humanity before the Fall. As long as we are in Christ Jesus, we no longer have to worry about working for our spiritual sustenance or suffering under the weight of earning our salvation.

Spirit Versus Flesh: The Great Contrast

One of the greatest understandings in Scripture is that Jesus has always wanted us to live in the spirit, not in the flesh. The Bible makes a crucial distinction between the "works of the flesh" and the "fruit of the Spirit."

When Scripture speaks of the works of the flesh (Galatians 5:19-21), it refers to them as exactly that—works. In other words, to commit anything in the flesh requires labor, effort, and toil. You must work the flesh to achieve fleshly desires. This is why the Bible declares: "For the wages of sin is death" (Romans 6:23). You only receive wages when you work.

For years, humanity has been working the flesh instead of resting in the Lord. But when the Bible talks about the fruit of the Spirit (Galatians 5:22-23), it refers to them as fruit—something that naturally grows and bears when you remain connected to the vine. As long as you are in Christ, you naturally bear the good fruits that God offers.

God's Redemptive Plan from the Beginning

Since the beginning of creation, God has been working to undo the mess that humanity created in the Garden of Eden. Instead of leaving us to labor endlessly for bread, He decided that He Himself would become the Bread of Life.

The Last Supper: The Ultimate Revelation

During the Last Supper, Jesus explained the profound mystery:

> *"And as they were eating, Jesus took bread, and blessed it, and brake it, and gave it to the disciples, and said, Take, eat; this is my body. And he took the cup, and gave thanks, and gave it to them, saying, "Drink ye all of it; For this is my blood of the new testament, which is shed for many for the remission of sins." - Matthew 26:26-28 (KJV)*

The bread represents His body, and the wine represents His blood. He instituted this during the Passover, which is profoundly significant—at the very feast commemorating Israel's deliverance from bondage, Jesus was establishing deliverance from the ultimate bondage of sin and death.

"Do This in Remembrance of Me"

When Jesus said, "This do in remembrance of me" (Luke 22:19), what exactly was He asking them to remember? Jesus had personally chosen these twelve disciples—tax collectors, fishermen, and others whom He hunted out individually. They all had issues, and they all had problems, but He was able to see the best in them. He sat with these people, ate with them, and told them, "Do this in remembrance of me."

Do what? Fellowship. Love one another. Share life together.

Beyond Ritual to Relationship

For years, we have thought that taking communion bread and wine once a month in church represented the Last Supper. But what Jesus was trying to establish was the love that had been demonstrated since the very beginning—when Abraham sat with the three men (a representation of the Father, the Son, and the Holy Spirit).

From the abundance of his heart, Abraham cooked, loved on them, sat with them, spoke with them, laughed with them, and fellowshipped with them. At that moment, they were eating, drinking, and fellowshipping together. Jesus wants us to do this in His remembrance.

Bread and Forgiveness: Inseparable Truths

Jesus' body has always been a representation of bread, and bread and forgiveness are synonymous in Scripture. You cannot have bread without forgiveness.

Remarkably, Bethlehem has a numeric value of 490 in Hebrew. In the New Testament, when Peter asked Jesus if he should forgive seven times, Jesus replied: "I say not unto thee, Until seven times: but, Until seventy times seven" (Matthew 18:22). Seventy times seven equals 490—the same numeric value as "bread" (lechem) in Hebrew.

What God is revealing is that you cannot have true bread without forgiveness. They are eternally linked.

The Heart of Divine Love

Jesus was willing and able to eat with the twelve disciples knowing that He was on His way to give His life on the cross. He was willing to sacrifice His life for humanity. "But God commendeth his love toward us, in that, while we were yet sinners, Christ died for us" (Romans 5:8).

This is what it means to feast with the Lord—getting together, loving one another, and doing what He did that day.

Love Despite Betrayal

Despite knowing that among His disciples there were those who would deny Him, betray Him with a kiss, and abandon their calling to return to their old lives, Jesus still loved them and cherished them. He demonstrated perfect love in the face of impending rejection and abandonment.

The Resurrection Breakfast

After Jesus' resurrection, He met Peter at the shoreline and said, "Cast the net on the right side of the ship" (John 21:6). Peter initially didn't recognize that it was Jesus speaking to him. After they cast the nets and caught an abundance of fish, Peter realized it was the Lord.

When Jesus got to the shore, there was food already prepared for Peter:

> *"As soon as they came to land, they saw a fire of coals there, and fish laid thereon, and bread... Jesus saith unto them, Come and dine" (John 21:9, 12).*

Notice the profound symbolism: there was fish being caught (representing the new ministry of being fishers of men), but Jesus was offering Himself as the bread. He was no longer just offering bread—He was saying, "If you want bread, then you want Jesus."

The fish represented the new path the Lord had provided. We no longer have to work for bread; we no longer have to sweat in anxiety and stress about what we're going to eat tomorrow.

Freedom from Tomorrow's Worries

In the book of Matthew, Jesus establishes this principle clearly:

> *"Therefore take no thought, saying, What shall we eat? or, What shall we drink? or, Where shall we be clothed? (For after all these things do the Gentiles seek:) for your heavenly Father knoweth that ye have need of all these things. But seek ye first the kingdom of God, and his righteousness; and all these things shall be added unto you. Take therefore no thought for the morrow: for the morrow shall take thought for the things of itself. Sufficient unto the day is the evil thereof." - Matthew 6:31-34 (KJV)*

Jesus establishes that worrying about tomorrow is what the Gentiles (those without God) do. But if we seek the kingdom of heaven and its righteousness, we shall inherit all these things.

What Are We Inheriting?

We are inheriting the assurance that God will provide all things—the same principle Moses established in the wilderness when Israel would wake up in the morning and eat fresh manna. We inherit freedom from the Genesis curse, freedom from anxiety about provision, and freedom from working for spiritual sustenance.

The Complete Circle

From Genesis 3:19's declaration that man would eat bread by the sweat of his brow, we have come full circle to Jesus declaring Himself the Bread of Life. The curse has been transformed into blessing, labor has been replaced by rest, and anxiety has been conquered by faith.

The Last Supper represents the ultimate fulfillment of every bread story in Scripture:

- **Manna** pointed to bread from heaven—Jesus is that bread
- **Abraham's hospitality** showed covenant fellowship—Jesus establishes the new covenant
- **David's table** demonstrated grace to the unworthy—Jesus welcomes all sinners
- **Joseph's provision** sustained nations during famine—Jesus sustains souls during spiritual famine

The Eternal Feast

When Jesus broke bread with His disciples and said, "Do this in remembrance of me," He was not instituting a ritual but inviting us into an eternal relationship. Every time we gather in His name, every time we share a meal with love and forgiveness, every time we fellowship with others as He did, we participate in the ongoing Last Supper.

The bread that once reminded us of our curse now reminds us of our salvation. The table that once required our labor now welcomes us as guests. The meal that once satisfied only temporarily now nourishes us eternally.

Jesus, the Bread of Life, born in Bethlehem (the house of bread), has become everything that humanity needed but could never provide for themselves. In Him, the long journey of bread through Scripture finds its perfect and eternal fulfillment.

6
The Marriage Supper of the Lamb

Revelation 19:6–9 — Where All Bread Stories Find Their Forever

The Table Was Always Set

You didn't start this book hungry by accident.

From the moment Adam's hands first broke ground to grow bread he was never meant to labor for, something deep in the human soul has been reaching toward a table it cannot yet see. Every meal in history — every shared loaf, every wilderness morning with manna on the ground, every Passover table, every communion cup — has been a whisper from eternity saying:

> *"This is not the feast. The feast is coming."*

And now, standing at the end of Scripture, we finally see what God was building all along.

> *"And I heard as it were the voice of a great multitude, and as the voice of many waters, and as the voice of mighty thunderings, saying, Alleluia: for the Lord God omnipotent reigneth. Let us be glad and rejoice, and give honour to him: for the marriage of the Lamb is come, and his wife hath made herself ready. And to her was granted that she should be arrayed in fine linen, clean and white: for the fine linen is the righteousness of saints. And he saith unto me, Write, Blessed are they which are called unto the marriage supper of the Lamb. And he saith unto me, These are the true sayings of God."*
>
> *— Revelation 19:6–9 (KJV)*

The Arc of the Whole Story

Every chapter of this study has been a single movement in one divine symphony. We did not trace the story of bread — we traced the story of God's relentless pursuit of His people through the most common thing on every table in human history.

The Bride and the Banquet

In Revelation, the Church is presented as the Bride of Christ, adorned in "fine linen, clean and white" — which the text itself tells us represents "the righteousness of saints." This bride has been preparing for this moment throughout all of human history. Every act of faith, every moment of fellowship, every communion table has been a rehearsal for this ultimate wedding feast.

The Marriage Supper represents the consummation of the relationship that began when God first walked with humanity in the Garden of Eden. What was lost in Genesis through disobedience is fully restored in Revelation through Christ's redemptive work. The garden that was closed becomes a city with open gates. The tree that was guarded by a flaming sword becomes freely accessible. The fellowship that was broken is not merely repaired — it is made eternal.

The Host Who Became the Meal

The profound beauty of this eternal feast is that the Host is the same One who became the meal.

Jesus, who broke His body as bread for our salvation, now hosts us at His eternal table. The Bread of Life who gave Himself as food for our souls now prepares the banquet for our eternal celebration. This is the ultimate reversal of the Genesis curse. Instead of humanity laboring for bread, the Bread Himself labors to prepare our feast. Instead of eating bread "by the sweat of thy brow," we feast by the blood of His brow — the drops that fell like blood in Gethsemane, and the crimson that flowed from the crown of thorns.

At this feast, He is both the Giver and the gift. Both the Provider and the provision. Both the Host and the holy meal.

All Nations at One Table

The vision of Revelation shows people from every tribe, tongue, and nation gathered at this feast:

> *"After this I beheld, and, lo, a great multitude, which no man could number, of all nations, and kindreds, and people, and tongues, stood before the throne, and before the Lamb, clothed with white robes, and palms in their hands."*
>
> *— Revelation 7:9 (KJV)*

This fulfills the promise implicit in Joseph's story, where all nations came to Egypt for bread during famine. Now, all nations come to the eternal Jerusalem for the eternal feast. The bread that once caused division — some nations having plenty while others starved — now creates unity as all feast equally at the Lamb's table. No hierarchy. No hunger. No outsiders. One table. One Host. One people.

The End of Hunger Forever

One of the most beautiful promises of this eternal feast is the permanent end of every hunger:

> *"They shall hunger no more, neither thirst any more; neither shall the sun light on them, nor any heat. For the Lamb which is in the midst of the throne shall feed them, and shall lead them unto living fountains of waters: and God shall wipe away all tears from their eyes."*
>
> *— Revelation 7:16–17 (KJV)*

The hunger that began in Genesis 3:19 — both physical and spiritual — finally ends forever. The Lamb who is the Bread of Life will personally feed His people for eternity. No more working for daily bread, no more anxiety about tomorrow's provision, no more spiritual famine or soul-emptiness. The cry that echoed from Eden across every wilderness of human suffering finally goes silent — not because the hunger is ignored, but because it is permanently satisfied.

The New Heaven and New Earth

> *"And I heard a great voice out of heaven saying, Behold, the tabernacle of God is with men, and he will dwell with them, and they shall be his people, and God himself shall be with them, and be their God. And God shall wipe away all tears from their eyes; and there shall be no more death, neither sorrow, nor crying, neither shall there be any more pain: for the former things are passed away."*
>
> *— Revelation 21:3–4 (KJV)*

In this new creation, the curse of Genesis 3 is not just reversed — it is completely dissolved. There will be no more pain from labor, no more sorrow from loss, no more death to separate loved ones from the feast. The "former things" — including the curse of eating bread by the sweat of our brow — have passed away forever. What God spoke in judgment in the garden, He removes in glory at the throne.

The Tree of Life Returns

> *"In the midst of the street of it, and on either side of the river, was there the tree of life, which bare twelve manner of fruits, and yielded her fruit every month: and the leaves of the tree were for the healing of the nations."*
>
> *— Revelation 22:2 (KJV)*

The tree that humanity was barred from accessing after the Fall is now freely available. But notice the layered beauty here: we don't just get the fruit of the Tree of Life — we get the Bread of Life as our eternal Host. What Adam lost by eating the wrong food, we gain by eating the right food: Christ Himself. Even the healing of the nations flows from leaves on the same tree. God wastes nothing. Every loss in Genesis is answered in Revelation with something greater than what was taken.

From Abraham's Tent to Heaven's Throne

The hospitality that began in Abraham's tent, where three divine visitors were welcomed with the finest bread and fellowship, reaches its ultimate expression in Heaven's throne room. Abraham's example of generous hospitality becomes the eternal reality as God hosts all His children at the grandest feast ever prepared.

David's table, where Mephibosheth's brokenness was covered and he was made equal with the king's sons, becomes the eternal table where all our brokenness is covered and we are made joint-heirs with Christ. Joseph's provision during famine, which saved nations from starvation, becomes the eternal provision where the Bread of Life satisfies all spiritual hunger forever.

Every table in Scripture was a shadow. This table is the substance.

The Invitation Still Extended

Even as Revelation describes this future feast, it stretches a hand toward every person who has not yet taken a seat:

> *"And the Spirit and the bride say, Come. And let him that heareth say, Come. And let him that is athirst come. And whosoever will, let him take the water of life freely."*
>
> *— Revelation 22:17 (KJV)*

The same Jesus who said "Come unto me, all ye that labour and are heavy laden" still calls people to His table. The invitation to the eternal feast is extended to all who thirst, all who hunger, all who will come freely. The door is not yet shut. The seat is not yet filled. The Host is still waiting.

Conclusion: The Bread That Became Everything

The same God who cursed the ground in Genesis 3 set a table in Revelation 19.

The same humanity that was expelled from the garden is invited to the banquet. And the Host — the One who broke His own body so we could eat — stands at the door of that feast with one word still on His lips:

"Come."

Notice who receives that invitation in Revelation 19:9. The Greek word translated "blessed" — *makarios* — is the same word Jesus used when He said, "Blessed are those who hunger and thirst for righteousness, for they shall be filled" (Matthew 5:6). The ones who sat on that hillside starving for something real, something eternal, something that would finally satisfy — those are the ones standing at the Marriage Supper.

God did not forget the hungry. He was preparing their table the whole time.

This is the ending of the bread story. Not a doctrine. Not a list. A *table*. A *feast*. A Groom who fought death itself to make sure His bride would not go hungry. A multitude so vast no man can number them — from every nation and tongue, people who once bent their backs under Genesis's curse — now seated, unashamed, full, and finally ***home***.

Until That Day

Until the Marriage Supper of the Lamb becomes reality, we continue to break bread in His remembrance.

Every time we say grace before a meal, we remember that all provision comes from God.

Every time we share communion, we proclaim Christ's death until He comes.

Every time we welcome someone to our table, we practice for eternity.

Every time we feed the hungry, we serve as His hands and feet.

Every time you break bread from this day forward, you are holding a piece of that story in your hands. Don't eat it casually.

The Transformation Complete

From Genesis to Revelation, from the curse to the celebration, the transformation is breathtaking:

The bread that began as a reminder of our mortality **has become the promise of our immortality.**

- *The bread that required our sweat* **has become the gift of His blood.**
- *The bread that separated us from paradise* **has become our invitation to paradise.**
- *The curse has become a blessing.* **The labor has become rest.**
- *The sweat has become celebration.* **The temporary has become eternal.**

The story of bread is the story of redemption.

The Bread That Became Everything

What began in Genesis as the result of sorrow and sweat has become, through Christ, the symbol of grace and eternal hope.

Bread began as a reminder of our fall:

that sin has consequences,

that life can be hard,

that provision requires labor,

and that humanity is deeply dependent.

But God never intended for the story to end in toil.

Through every generation, He was revealing something greater:

that physical hunger was always pointing to a deeper hunger—

the hunger of the soul.

And then Jesus came.

He stepped into our world not merely to teach truth, but to become truth made flesh.

He was born in Bethlehem—the House of Bread—

because He came to satisfy what nothing else ever could.

He became:

- the manna in our wilderness,
- the bread at our table,
- the grace that covers our shame,
- the provision in famine,
- the body broken for our healing,
- and the eternal feast awaiting us in glory.

Because of Christ:

- our labor becomes rest,
- our fear becomes trust,
- our emptiness becomes fullness,
- and our temporary hunger becomes eternal satisfaction.

This is not just a study about bread.

This is a revelation of the heart of God.

Every loaf,

every table,

every communion,

every shared meal—

points us back to Jesus.

The Bread that once symbolized survival

now symbolizes salvation.

The Bread that once reminded us of death

now reminds us of eternal life.

And until that glorious day when we sit at the Marriage Supper of the Lamb,

we continue to remember:

He is enough.

He always has been.

He always will be.

Suggested Biblical Reference Section
(for back matter or study guide)

Key Scriptures Used in This Book:

- Genesis 3:19
- Genesis 18:1–8
- Exodus 16:4–32
- Exodus 25:30
- 1 Samuel 21:6
- 2 Samuel 9:1–13
- Psalm 23:5
- Genesis 37–41
- Matthew 6:31–34
- Matthew 11:28–30
- Matthew 26:26–28
- Luke 22:19
- John 6:35
- John 21:9–12
- Revelation 7:16–17
- Revelation 19:6–9
- Revelation 22:17

About the Author

Osvaldo Feliciano was born and raised in the Bronx, New York, where his journey of faith began at the age of nine when his father gave his heart to Jesus in 1994. After spending his formative years in New York, he moved to Virginia, where he graduated from Kecoughtan High School in Hampton, and he now calls Millville, New Jersey home.

Osvaldo has been immersed in the life of the church for as long as he can remember. In 2015, after two years of dedicated training, study, and service, he received his certificate of ministry under the covering of his father, Pastor Ramon Feliciano, and Bishop William McCarty — a milestone that reflected not just a title, but a life surrendered to the Word of God.

For most of his life, reading did not come easy. It wasn't until the age of twenty-one that he picked up his first book, and it took great effort to finish it. But when he turned to the Bible, everything changed. The Word came alive — vivid, moving, breathing — and he could not stop. He learned that the secret was not just in reading, but in pausing, reflecting, and allowing the Spirit of God to transform the heart.

The Bread was born out of that same rhythm. A question first stirred at eighteen — "why is bread part of a curse?" — quietly baked in his heart for years, surfacing through studies, sermons, and seasons of life, including a season spent attending a church fittingly called the House of Bread. What began as a question in Genesis became a journey through the entirety of Scripture, and by 2024, the writing began. By 2025, the book was complete.

Osvaldo writes for the curious — for those who, like him, long to understand not just what the Bible says, but where it all begins and why it matters. His prayer is simple: that every reader would slow down, pause, and let the Word of God come alive in them too.

www.ingramcontent.com/pod-product-compliance
Lightning Source LLC
LaVergne TN
LVHW090616110826
845146LV00001B/411

* 9 7 9 8 9 9 5 8 0 5 4 3 4 *